# Mutual Fund Investments

## Best of the Best

## 2nd Edition

www.largedividends.com/mutual-fund-performance.html

## Disclaimer Notice:

The author compiled the information provided herein from various sources.   Every effort has been taken to provide accurate, reliable,   and complete information within this book.   The author does not assume, and hereby disclaims liability for any loss, damage, or hurt caused by possible human error.   There are no guarantees of future results of the mutual funds listed herein.

# INTRODUCTION

This Kindle book provides valuable information that helps you achieve your goals of prosperity from your portfolio investments.

The factual data, herein, includes **25 profitable mutual funds** that far exceed the average performance of the respective investment category. Every mutual fund is ranked* in the top 10% or top 20%. These investments are the best of the best because of these returns on investments:

- 2018 year-end ranked top 10%/top 20% **2.36% average return.**
- 3-year annualized return ranked top 10%/ top 20% **10.88% average annualized return**.

- 5-year annualized return ranked top 10%/ top 20% **8.04% average annualized return**.
  *Source: The Wall Street Journal quarterly mutual funds listing

Making use of 3 profitable mutual funds, an excellent model was created in the Financial Wealth section to illustrate how to build wealth for savings or retirement. This investment formula includes 9 years of mutual fund investments.

# TABLE of CONTENTS:

**RETIREMENT**................................................ 1

   Commitment...........................................2

   Establishing Goal..................................3

   Perseverance........................................4

**INDIVIDUAL RETIREMENT ACCT 101**...........5

   Definition of a IRA................................ 6

   Contribution limits...............................7

   Withholding calculator........................... 7

   Contribution after 70½ years of age...........7

   Claiming IRA tax deduction.....................7

   Required Minimum Distribution...............8

   Rollover guideline.................................8

**MUTUAL FUNDS 101**...............................10

   Definition of a mutual fund....................11

   Bond Mutual Fund................................ 12

   Dollar-Cost-Averaging........................... 18

   Income/Capital Gains Distribution........... 17

   Investment Facts..................................19

   Market Capitalization............................16

   Profile................................................14

   Performance........................................15

   Profitable Return Formula......................18

   Purchase.............................................15

   Return................................................15

    Risk.................................................16

    Stock/Equity Mutual Funds....................13

    Top Holdings....................................16

**MUTUAL FUND FINANCIAL REPORTS**

**Core Bond**

    Mutual fund......................................23

    2018  return.....................................24

    5-year average returns........................25

    2019  performance.............................26

**Convertible Securities**

    Mutual fund......................................27

    2018 return......................................28

    5–years average returns......................29

    2019 performance.............................30

**Equity Income**

    Mutual fund......................................31

    2018 return......................................32

    5–years average returns......................33

    2019 performance.............................34

**Flexible Portfolio**

    Mutual fund......................................35

    2018 return......................................36

    5–years average returns......................37

    2019 performance.............................38

**General & Insured Municipal**

    Mutual fund......................................39

2018 return..................................................40

5-years average returns........................41

2019 performance................................42

**Global Small/Mid-Cap**

Mutual fund...........................................43

2018 return..........................................44

5-years average returns........................45

2019 performance................................46

**Health & Bio-Technology**

Mutual fund...........................................47

2018 return..........................................48

5-years average returns........................49

2019 performance................................50

**High Yield Municipal**

Mutual fund...........................................51

2018 return..........................................52

5-years average returns........................53

2019 performance................................54

**Intermediate Municipal Debt**

Mutual fund...........................................55

2018 return..........................................56

5-years average returns........................57

2019 performance................................58

**Large-Cap Core**

Mutual fund...........................................59

2018 return..........................................60

5-years average returns...............................61

2019 performance......................................62

**Large-Cap Growth**

Mutual fund...............................................63

2018 return...............................................64

5-years average returns.............................65

2019 performance......................................66

**Large-Cap Value**

Mutual fund...............................................67

2018 return............................................... 68

5-years average return..............................69

2019 performance ..................................... 70

**Mid-Cap Core**

Mutual fund............................................... 71

2018 return............................................... 72

5-years average return.............................. 73

2019 performance...................................... 74

**Mid-Cap Growth**

Mutual fund...............................................75

2018 return............................................... 76

5-years average return.............................. 77

2019 performance...................................... 78

**Mixed-Asset Target Alloc: Conservative**

Mutual fund...............................................79

2018 return...............................................80

5-years average return...............................81

2019 performance..................................... 82

**Mixed–Asset Target Allocation: Growth**

Mutual fund..............................................83

2018 return..............................................84

5–years average return........................... 85

2019 performance....................................86

**Mixed–Asset Target Allocation: Moderate**

Mutual fund..............................................87

2018 return..............................................88

5–years average return............................89

2019 performance....................................90

**Multi–Cap Growth**

Mutual fund..............................................91

2018 return..............................................92

5–years average return............................93

2019 performance....................................94

**Multi–Cap Value**

Mutual fund..............................................95

2018 return.............................................. 96

5–years average return............................97

2019 performance....................................98

**Small–Cap Core**

Mutual fund..............................................99

2018 return............................................. 100

5–years average return........................... 101

2019 performance.................................... 102

## Small-Cap Growth

Mutual fund............................................103

2018 return............................................104

5-years average return.........................105

2019 performance.................................106

## Small-Cap Value

Mutual fund............................................107

2018 return............................................108

5-years average return.........................109

2019 performance.................................110

## Telecommunications

Mutual fund............................................ 111

2018 return............................................ 112

5-years average return......................... 113

2019 performance................................. 114

## United States Mortgage

Mutual fund............................................ 115

2018 return............................................ 116

5-years average return......................... 117

2019 performance................................. 118

## Utility

Mutual fund............................................119

2018 return............................................120

5-years average return......................... 121

2019 performance................................. 122

## FINANCIAL WEALTH

Initial Investment......................................123
Second Investment..................................128
Third Investment....................................129
Portfolio Prosperity................................130

# Excerpt of Large–Cap Core mutual fund 2019 performance on page 62.

## There are  mutual funds in this category:

|                      | Fund   | Category |         |
| -------------------- | ------ | -------- | ------- |
| **Category**<br>**As of: 3/15/19** | **Return** | **Average** | **\*Rank** |
| **Year-to-date**     | 18.29% | 12.56%   | 2%      |
| **1-year**           | 12.88% | 3.45%    | 1%      |
| **3-year annualized**| 22.61% | 12.89%   | 1%      |
| **5-year annualized**| 13.82% | 9.54%    | 1%      |

Source: Wall Street Journal             *1% Best – 100% Worst

# RETIREMENT

If you are a middle aged wage earner, or older, invest in one of the best types of investment portfolios to build a nest egg, an Individual Retirement Account (IRA). Time waits for no one! Every year we are getting a little older. It is essential to plan for the future and prepare for your retirement now, not tomorrow. This can best be achieved by establishing a goal, making a commitment, and persevering to achieve the goal.

**Establishing Goal**: Your first important consideration to making an investment is to consider what type of mutual fund investment objective you want in your portfolio. The objective can be aggressive, conservative or moderate.

Aggressive is a method to achieve maximum returns. An aggressive investment strategy attempts to grow assets at above-average rate compared to its industry or the overall market

Conservative is an investment strategy that aims to grow invested capital over the long-term. This strategy focuses on minimizing risk by making long-term investments in companies that show consistent growth over time. Conservative growth mutual funds have low asset turnover or a high percentage of fixed assets on the balance sheets and use a buy-hold investment strategy.

Moderate investments try to reduce risks and increase returns equally. The investment may incur a short-term loss of principal and lower degree of liquidity in exchange for long-term appreciation.

**Commitment**: To achieve your objectives for retirement, prosperity, you must establish a goal and not deviate from it. You have to decide on the amount of money that will be saved and invested in your retirement portfolio and how often. After making the minimum investment in a mutual fund, you can make weekly, bi-weekly, monthly or annual additional investment payments to reach the, the allowable IRA maximum.

**Perseverance:** Most times, it is difficult to save money; especially when you encounter hard times due to illness, expenses, etc. You have to be persistent in saving as much money as possible and stay committed to your personal goal.

# INDIVIDUAL RETIREMENT ACCOUNT
## 101

Here is a narrative describing what an Individual Retirement Account is, important investment terms to understand and be familiar with.

Individual Retirement Accounts are one of the best investment options available to individuals for a retirement portfolio You are always in complete control of your investments. You determine what risk will be taken to achieve the investment success you want in your portfolio. You decide whether the investment is aggressive, moderate, or conservative. You invest in the mutual fund category that you determine will best fit your needs. You determine how much money will be invested and how often.

An Individual Retirement Account is a great way to save for the future! Did you know all mutual fund income/capital gains distribution that you reinvested is not taxable income until you reach the age of 70½? Of course, if you do not reinvest the distribution, all income capital gains received are taxable.

Contribution Limits: For 2019, the maximum you can contribute to all of your traditional and Roth IRA is $5500, if you are under 50. The maximum is $6500, for individuals who are 50 years of age or older.

IRS Withholding Calculator: This easy-to-use calculator can help you determine your annual federal income tax withholding so that your employer can withhold the correct amount from your salary. This is particularly helpful if you had:

- excess money withheld in the past
- your situation changed
- to start a new job.

Contribution after age $70\frac{1}{2}$: You cannot make regular contributions to a traditional IRA if you are $70\frac{1}{2}$ or older. However; you can still contribute to a Roth IRA and make rollover contributions to a Roth IRA regardless of your age.

Claiming tax deduction: Any IRA losses on your tax return cannot be reported while the IRA is still open.

Rollovers: Are now limited to making only one rollover each year. If you make a rollover, you must rollover money withdrawn from one investment into another investment within 60 days from date of withdrawal.

Source: Internal Revenue Service: https://www.irs.gov/retirement-plans/traditional-and-roth-iras

Once you reach 70½ years of age, you must withdraw a minimum amount of distribution from your IRA portfolio every year. You reach age 70½ on the date that is six calendar months after your 70th birthday.

The Required Minimum Distribution calculates the total withdraw that must be taken for the IRS tax year. Than you must make withdraws as posted in your RMD account. Example: You are retired and your 70th birthday was June 30, 2017. You reached age 70½ on December 30, 2017. You must take your first RMD (for 2017) by April 1, 2018.

You decide which mutual fund investments to make withdrawals from. RMD withdrawals can be made from several IRA accounts in your portfolio as long as the total withdraws equal the RMD calculation for that year.

Note: If you <u>do not withdraw</u> the minimum calculated RMD, you will be subject to severe penalties. Investors with diversified mutual funds, are informed by each mutual fund as to the amount of distribution to be withdrawn for the current year.

The RMD calculator for 2019 analyzes:

1. Account owner's date of birth (month, day, & year)
2. IRA **total retirement balance** as of December 31, 2019
3. Expected annual rate of return (%)
4. Beneficiary type (e.g. spouse)
5. Beneficiary's birthday (month, day, year)

# MUTUAL FUNDS

Here is a narrative describing what are mutual funds and important investment terms to understand and be familiar with.

A mutual fund in the United States is an investment that is regulated by the Securities & Exchange Commission and usually listed on the NASDAQ market. Being an investment company, a mutual fund is in the business of collecting funds from investors and pooling the assets for the purpose of building a portfolio of securities according to stated objectives in the prospectus. The objectives determine the financial category and risk.

Mutual funds are long-term investments for building assets in IRAs and should be timed in years not months or weeks. A mutual fund's portfolio is structured and maintained to achieve the investment objectives that are in its prospectus. Before investing in a mutual fund, you want to know the year-to-date performance, the returns for the long-term, the income and/or capital gains distribution, and the risk.

Your objective of making investments should result in maximizing gains in a positive market and minimizing losses in a negative market. Being a prudent investor, you want to assure continued mutual fund successes. To accomplish this, you have to be a committed investor for the long-term.

The two types of mutual funds presented in this book are:

1. Stock/Equity are mutual funds that purchase securities from companies and industries that are listed on Dow Jones, NASDAQ, Russell Index.

2. Bond mutual funds are invested primarily in United States bonds and/or other debt securities.

Mutual funds are not guaranteed by the government or FDIC. There are no guarantees of future performance. A healthy and prosperous portfolio can best be achieved on proven long-term positive years of gains compared to years of losses. The performance gains, distribution of income and/or capital gains will affect the success or failure of your retirement investments.

Before making an investment, consideration should be given to mutual fund fees, the minimum required purchase, market risk, investment categories, etc.

All tools of the trade allow individuals, in all professions, to excel in the profession. One of the best tools available in the financial field is using a mutual fund's ticker symbol. The ticker symbol is your key to valuable investment facts. As an example: You would use the ticker symbol FATRX for Frost Total Bond Fund.

The data below gives you a glimpse of valuable resources that are unlocked using a mutual fund's ticker symbol. This is the vital information you need to secure and build a prosperous financial portfolio for your future.

Profile: Lists the mutual fund's family,

address, toll free phone number, portfolio manager's name and tenure, fund's inception date, fund's net assets, investment fund category and objectives.

Purchase: Includes the mutual fund's minimum initial purchase, minimum initial IRA purchase, minimum subsequent purchases, maximum 12b1 fee and maximum front and sales load (if any).

Performance: The percentage of gain or loss of the fund's net asset value (share price). The gain or loss is determined by the difference of the opening price vs. the closing price. The net asset value is the current market price of the mutual fund assets per share. The net asset value is reduced by the amount of distribution or performance loss.

Return: Includes the dividend distribution of income or capital gains and the performance of the mutual fund. The distribution of income is usually declared quarterly, i.e. March, June, September and December. Many mutual capital gains during the month of December.

On the day of trade, the share price is decreased by the same amount of distribution (dividends or capital gains) given to shareholders. If, for example a two dollar distribution is declared, the net asset value of the mutual fund is reduced by two dollars at the close of the market.

Top Holdings: Provides the top 10 holdings by name of investment and the percent of assets purchased. Asset allocations include portfolio percentage of stocks, cash and bonds are provided. You see the type of assets included like technology, health care, banking, etc.

Risk: Shows the risk level of a mutual fund attempt to achieve its investment objective. Is the fund a low risk, below risk, average risk, above average risk, or a high risk? The 3–year and 5–year alpha and beta risk rating are also included.

Market Capitalization (Cap) indicates the size and value of the company's stock that the mutual fund invests in and are included in the portfolio. Large–Caps are big companies with sales over $10 billion. Mid–Cap are companies with sales between $2 billion and $10 billion. Multi–cap sales are between $2 billion and over $10 billion. Small–Cap includes small size companies whose sales are below $2 billion.

Income/Capital Gains Distribution: Shareholders who receive mutual fund distributions have the option to reinvest the income and/or the capital gains to avoid paying tax, when it is an IRA account. Any distribution paid to the holder is is taxable.

A fund sells an investment security for a higher price than originally paid results in a capital gain. A capital loss is realized when the fund sells an investment security for a lower price than originally paid.

If the investment security is held by the fund for more than one year, the gain or loss will be a long-term capital gain or loss. If the investment security is held by the fund for less than one year, the gain or loss will be a short-term capital gains and losses.

Mutual fund gains or losses are netted together and when the fund has a net gain, that increase is distributed to the shareholder once a year. By law, mutual funds must pay out income and realized capital gains to shareholders. These types of distribution are taken from the fund's assets which results in the net asset value being reduced by the same amount as the distribution pay out.

Dollar-cost-averaging: This type of investment occurs when you invest at regular intervals, regardless of the market conditions being up or down. This action is beneficial in the long-term because you are purchasing shares at different prices which reflect the ups and downs of the market.

Profitable Return Formula: Mutual funds that are profitable and exceptional, all 25 mutual funds listed in this book, have included the following criteria:

- Consistent above average performance

- Top investment category ranking
- Since inception, more years of gains and fewer years of losses

Investment Facts: Can be easily verified once you read the mutual fund's prospectus. Most Internet financial search engines provide information that you need, which is based on facts. To view the vast resources of mutual fund data, use the fund's ticker symbol. A financial search engine like Yahoo or Google simply requires the ticker symbol being placed into the QUOTE dialog box.

# MUTUAL FUND FINANCIAL REPORTS
## (2014 thru 2018)

Here are successful Stock/Equity and Bond mutual fund reports. All investments are open-end mutual funds. There is no guarantee of completeness or accuracy of the researched mutual fund data* of distribution, performances and returns which are based on the last market closing date in December of each year.

There is no guarantee of future results. The financial reports are not offered to buy or sell a particular fund. There is no guarantee of future results. Always contact the mutual fund and read the prospectus before making any investment decision.
*Source: Yahoo, Market Watch, Barons, Lipper, Morningstar, Wall Street Journal

Year-to-date, 3-year & 5-year annualized returns of these mutual funds are posted weekly on the website www.largedividends.com/mutual-fund-performance.html.

Investment Fund Category:
**Core Bond**

The Fund seeks a high and stable rate of current income, consistent with long-term preservation of capital. A secondary objective is to take advantage of opportunities to realize capital appreciation.

As the December 31, 2018, the average return performance for this category is −0.69%. This mutual fund's return is 1.15% compared to 604 total mutual funds.

**Frost Total Bond Fund (FATRX)**
877-713-7678
www.frostbank.com

Advisors Inner Circle Fund II
100 West Houston Street
San Antonio, TX 78205

Risk: high

Minimum Investment Purchase: $2500
Minimum IRA Purchase: $1500
Maximum Front End Sales Load: No Load
Date of Inception: June 30, 2008
Number of Years of Gains: 9
Number of Years of Losses: 1
Net Expense Ratio: 0.73%
Category Average Net Expense Ratio: 0.73%
Open to all investors

**TOTAL ASSETS**: $3.08 billion

**NET ASSET ALLOCATION:**

Cash: 2.46%
Stock: 0.07%
Bonds: 97.35%
Other: 0.03%

### FIVE YEAR RETURNS:

**Year: 2018**
Net Asset Value: $10.20   –2.11%
Distribution: $.34   3.26%
Total Return: 1.15%

## Year: 2017

Net Asset Value: $10.42    0.68%
Distribution: $.36    3.48%
Total Return: 4.16%

## Year: 2016

Net Asset Value: $10.35    1.47%
Distribution: $.39    3.82%
Total Return: 5.29%

## Year: 2015

Net Asset Value: $10.20    -4.40%
Distribution: $.39    3.66%
Total Return: -0.75%

## Year: 2014

Net Asset Value: $10.67    4.49%
Distribution: $.52    4.86%
Total Return: 4.49%

## ANNUAL AVERAGE RETURNS:

5-year average distribution: 3.82%
5-year average performance: -0.95%
5-year average return: 2.87%

3-year average distribution: 3.52%
3-year average performance: -0.01%
3-year average return: 3.53%

2-year average distribution: 3.37%
2-year average performance: -0.72%
2-year average return: 2.65%

There are 604 mutual funds in this category:

| As of: 3/15/19 | Fund Return | Category Average | Category *Rank |
|---|---|---|---|
| Year-to-date | 1.72% | 2.44% | 89% |
| 1-year | 3.41% | 3.25% | 39% |
| 3-year annualized | 4.01% | 3.05% | 14% |
| 5-year annualized | 2.75% | 2.50% | 35% |

Source: Wall Street Journal                    *1% Best – 100% Worst

Before making an investment, always read the mutual fund prospective.

Investment Category:
**Convertible Securities**

The Fund seeks to maximize total return, consistent with reasonable risk, by seeking to optimize capital appreciation and high current income under varying market conditions. The Fund normally invests at least 80% of its net assets in convertible securities.

As the December 31, 2018, the average return for this category is -1.91%. This mutual fund's return is -1.00% compared to 82 total mutual funds.

**Columbia Convertible Securities A  (PACIX)**
800-345-6611
www.columbiathreadneedleus.com

Columbia Funds Series Trust
One Financial Center
Boston MA 02111

Risk: above-average

Minimum Investment Purchase: $2000
Minimum IRA Purchase: $1000
Maximum Front End Sales Load: 5.75%
Date of Inception: September 25, 1987
Number of Years of Gains: 23
Number of Years of Losses: 8
Net Expense Ratio: 1.12%
Category Average Net Expense Ratio: 1.27%
Open to all investors

**TOTAL ASSETS:** $931.76 million

**NET ASSET ALLOCATION:**

Cash: 0.72%
Stock: 6.07%
Bonds: 0.00%
Other: 1.76%
Preferred Securities: 13.80%
Convertible Securities: 77.65%

## FIVE YEAR RETURNS:

Year: 2018
Net Asset Value: $18.76   –5.78%
Distribution: $.95   4.78%

Total Return: -1.00%

Year: 2017
Net Asset Value: $19.91   11.85%
Distribution: $.57   3.22%
Total Return: 15.07%

Year: 2016
Net Asset Value: $17.80   8.60%
Dividend Distribution: $.42   2.54%
Total Return: 11.14%

Year: 2015
Net Asset Value: $16.39   -12.91%
Dividend Distribution: $1.57   8.34%
Total Return: -4.57%

Year: 2014
Net Asset Value: $18.82   3.52%
Dividend Distribution: $.89   4.92%
Total Return: 8.44%

**ANNUAL AVERAGE RETURNS:**

5-year average distribution: 4.76%
5-year average performance: 1.06%

5-year average return: 5.82%

3-year average distribution: 3.51%
3-year average performance: 4.89%
3-year average return: 8.40%

2-year average distribution: 4.00%
2-year average performance: 3.04%
2-year average return: 7.04%

There are 82 mutual funds in this category:

| As of: 3/15/19 | Fund Return | Category Average | Category *Rank |
|---|---|---|---|
| Year-to-date | 11.99% | 10.75% | 23% |
| 1-year | 5.42% | 3.65% | 25% |
| 3-year annualized | 14.49% | 11.40% | 12% |
| 5-year annualized | 6.96% | 5.78% | 26% |

Source: Wall Street Journal          *1% Best – 100% Worst

Before making an investment, always get the mutual fund prospective.

## Investment Fund Category:
### Equity Income

Fund's objective seeks current income and long–term growth of common stocks middle size in large size companies usually pay above-average dividend income and yet, undervalued relative to other stocks. Usually the fund will invest minimum of 80% of its assets in equity securities.

As the December 31, 2018, the average return for this category is -7.24%. This mutual fund's return is 2.09% compared to 596 total mutual funds.

**FAM Equity-Income Investor (FAMEX)**
800-225-6292
www.famfunds.com

Fenimore Asset Management Trust
384 N Grand St, Po Box 399
Cobleskill NY 12043

Risk: low
Minimum Investment Purchase: $500
Minimum IRA Purchase: $1200
Maximum Front End Sales Load: none
Date of Inception: April 1, 1996
Number of Years of Gains: 17
Number of Years of Losses: 5
Net Expense Ratio: 1.25% %
Category Average Net Expense Ratio: 1.06%
Open to all investors

**TOTAL ASSETS**: $240.55 million

**NET ASSET ALLOCATION:**

Cash: 0.07%
Stock: 91.33%
Bonds: 0.00%
Other: 0.00%

### FIVE YEAR RETURNS:

Year: 2018
Net Asset Value: $29.73   –1.26%
Dividend Distribution: $1.01    3.35%
Total Return: 2.09%

Year: 2017
Net Asset Value: $30.11   11.81%
Dividend Distribution: $.21   0.78%
Total Return: 12.59%

Year: 2016
Net Asset Value: $26.93   11.70%
Dividend Distribution: $2.36   9.79%
Total Return: 21.49%

Year: 2015
Net Asset Value: $24.11   −5.56%
Dividend Distribution: $1.25   4.90%
Total Return: −0.66%

Year: 2014
Net Asset Value: $25.53   3.07%
Dividend Distribution: $1.18   4.78%
Total Return: 7.85%

**ANNUAL AVERAGE RETURNS:**
5-year average distribution: 4.72%
5-year average performance: 3.95%
5-year average return: 8.67%

3-year average distribution: 4.64%

3-year average performance: 7.42%
3-year average return: 12.06%

2–year average distribution: 2.07%
2-year average performance: 5.27%
2-year average return: 7.34%

There are 596 mutual funds in this category:

| As of: 3/15/19 | Fund Return | Category Average | Category *Rank |
|---|---|---|---|
| Year-to-date | 14.19% | 10.95% | 3% |
| 1-year | 14.52% | 3.00% | 1% |
| 3-year annualized | 11.52% | 10.41% | 2% |
| 5-year annualized | 16.11% | 7.70% | 5% |

Source: Wall Street Journal                    *1% Best – 100% Worst

Before making an investment, always read the mutual fund prospective.

Investment Fund Category:
**Flexible Portfolio**

Fund's objective is to acquire long–term capital appreciation. Invest primarily in domestic common stocks and bonds, including "zero-coupon" government bonds.

As the December 31, 2018, the average return for this category is -7.31%. This mutual fund's return is -3.58% compared to 662 total mutual funds.

**Meeder Muirfield Retail (FLMFX)**
800-325-3539
www.meeder.com

Meeder Funds
6125 Memorial Dr., PO Box 7177
Dublin, OH 43017

Risk: Above Average
Minimum Investment Purchase: $2500
Minimum IRA Purchase: $500

Maximum Front End Sales Load: None
Date of Inception: August 3, 1988
Number of Years of Gains: 23
Number of Years of Losses: 7
Net Expense Ratio: 1.27%
Category Average Net Expense Ratio: 1.38%
Open to all investors

**TOTAL ASSETS**: $610.05 million

**NET ASSET ALLOCATION**:
Cash: 56.95%
Stock: 43.05% %
Bonds: 0.00%
Other: 0.00%

### FIVE YEAR RETURNS:

Year: 2018
Net Asset Value: $7.16   -5.04%
Distribution: $.11   1.46%
Total Return: -3.58%


Year: 2017
Net Asset Value: $7.54   10.23%
Distribution: $.69   10.07%

Total Return: 20.30%

Year: 2016
Net Asset Value: $6.84   5.72%
Distribution: $.06     0.93%
Total Return: 6.65%

Year: 2015
Net Asset Value: $6.47   -7.97%
Distribution: $.17   2.42%
Total Return: -5.55%

Year: 2014
Net Asset Value: $7.03   1.15%
Distribution: $.06     0.82%
Total Return: 1.97%

## ANNUAL AVERAGE RETURNS:

5-year average distribution: 3.14%
5-year average performance: 0.82%
5-year average return: 3.96%

3-year average distribution: 4.15%
3-year average performance: -0.93%
3-year average return: 3.22%

2–year average distribution: 5.77%

2-year average performance: 2.60%

2-year average return: 8.37%

There are 662 mutual funds in this category:

| As of: 3/15/19 | Fund Return | Category Average | Category *Rank |
|---|---|---|---|
| Year-to-date | 3.49% | 7.32% | 88% |
| 1-year | -2.11% | -0.87% | 70% |
| 3-year annualized | 9.14% | 6.44% | 12% |
| 5-year annualized | 6.11% | 3.43% | 9% |

Source: Wall Street Journal                    *1% Best – 100% Worst

Before making an investment, always read the mutual fund prospective.

Investment Fund Category:
**General and Insured Municipal Debt**

The fund's objective is to maximize current income that is exempt from federal income taxes and preserve investors principal. The fund invests at least 80% of its assets in long-term investment grade municipal bonds, with ratings of Baa or higher. The remaining 20% are invested in bonds that are rated less than Baa or are unrated.

As the December 31, 2018, the average return for this category is 0.68%. This mutual fund's return is 7.34% compared to  80 total mutual funds.

**Oppenheimer Rochester AMT  (OPTAX)**
800-225-5677
www.oppenheimerfunds.com

Oppenheimer AMT–Free Municipal's
6803 South Tucson Way
Centennial, CO 80112–3924

Risk: high
Minimum Investment Purchase: $1000
Minimum IRA Purchase: $500
Maximum Front End Sales Load: 4.75%
Date of Inception: October 26, 1976
Number of Years of Gains: 32
Number of Years of Losses: 10
Net Expense Ratio: 1.03%
Category Average Net Expense Ratio: 0.95%
Open to all investors

**TOTAL ASSETS**: $1.88 billion

**NET ASSET ALLOCATION**:
Cash: 0.50%
Stock: 0.00%
Bonds: 99.50%

### FIVE YEAR RETURNS:

Year: 2018
Net Asset Value: $7.04   3.38%
Distribution: $.27   3.96%
Total Return: 7.34%

Year: 2017

Net Asset Value: $6.81   1.19%
Distribution: $.32   4.77%
Total Return: 5.96%


Year: 2016
Net Asset Value: $6.73   -3.03%
Distribution: $.38   5.50%
Total Return: 2.47%


Year: 2015
Net Asset Value: $6.94   -1.00%
Distribution: $.43   6.19%
Total Return: 5.19%


Year: 2014
Net Asset Value: $7.01   9.02%
Distribution: $.42   6.58%
Total Return: 15.60%

**ANNUAL AVERAGE RETURNS:**

5-year average distribution: 5.40%
5-year average performance: 1.91%
5-year average return: 7.31%

3-year average distribution: 4.74%
3-year average performance: 0.51% %
3-year average return: 5.25%

2-year average distribution: 4.36%
2-year average performance: 2.29%
2-year average return: 6.65%

There are 80 mutual funds in this category:

| As of: 3/15/19 | Fund Return | Category Average | Category *Rank |
|---|---|---|---|
| Year-to-date | 3.25% | 1.81% | 1% |
| 1-year | 10.22% | 3.94% | 1% |
| 3-year annualized | 5.93% | 2.40% | 1% |
| 5-year annualized | 6.50% | 3.43% | 1% |

Source: Wall Street Journal          *1% Best – 100% Worst

Before making an investment, always read the mutual fund prospective.

Investment Fund Category:
**Global Small–Cap/Mid–Cap**

The Fund seeks to provide shareholders with long-term growth of capital by investing in equity securities of domestic and foreign small/cap/mid-cap companies that provide good valuation opportunities.

As the December 31, 2018, the average return for this category is -12.72%. This mutual fund's return is 0.29%.

**Kinetics Small Cap Opportunities (KSCOX)**
800-930-3828
www.kineticsfunds.com

Kinetics Mutual Funds, Inc.
555 Taxter Road - Suite 175
Sleepy Hollow NY 10591

Risk: average
Minimum Investment Purchase: $2500

Minimum IRA Purchase: $2500
Maximum Front End Sales Load: none
Date of Inception: March 20, 2000
Number of Years of Gains: 13
Number of Years of Losses: 5
Net Expense Ratio: 1.64%
Category Average Net Expense Ratio: 1.16%
Open to investors

**TOTAL ASSETS**: $223.6 million

**NET ASSET ALLOCATION:**
Cash: 31.14%
Stock: 65.25%
Bond: 0.00%
Other: 3.29%
Preferred Securities: 0.32%

### FIVE YEAR RETURNS:

Year: 2018
Net Asset Value: $51.40   0.29%
Distribution: $0.00
Total Return: 0.29%

Year: 2017

Net Asset Value: $51.25    26.23%
Distribution: $0.00
Total Return: 26.23%


Year: 2016
Net Asset Value: $40.60    24.39%
Distribution: $0.00
Total Return: 24.39%


Year: 2015
Net Asset Value: $32.64    -12.26%
Distribution: $0.00
Total Return: -12.26%


Year: 2014
Net Asset Value: $37.20    -7.28%
Distribution: $0.00
Total Return: -7.28%

## ANNUAL AVERAGE RETURNS:

5-year average distribution: 0.00%
5-year average performance: 6.28%
5-year average return: 6.28%

3-year average distribution: 0.00%

3-year average performance: 16.97%
3-year average return: 16.97%

2–year average distribution: 0.00%
2-year average performance: 13.26%
2-year average return: 13.26%

| As of: 3/15/19 | Fund Return | Category Average | Category *Rank |
|---|---|---|---|
| Year-to-date | 17.78% | 13.71% | 9% |
| 1-year | 10.17% | -4.39% | 2% |
| 3-year annualized | 13.32% | 12.27% | 2% |
| 5-year annualized | 8.34% | 5.48% | 11% |

Source: Wall Street Journal          *1% Best – 100% Worst

Before making an investment, always read the mutual fund prospective.

Investment Fund Category:
**Health/Bio-Technology**

Fund's objective seeks capital appreciation by investing in equity securities of companies related to healthcare, medicine and bio technology.

As the December 31, 2018, the average return for this category is -0.89%. This mutual fund's return is 10.72% compared to 75 total mutual funds.

**Fidelity Select Health Care Services (FSHCX)**
800-544-8544
www.institutionalfidelity.com

Fidelity Select Portfolios
82 Devonshire Street
Boston MA 02109

Risk: average
Minimum Investment Purchase: $0

Minimum IRA Purchase: $2500
Maximum Front End Sales Load: No Load
Date of Inception: June 30, 1986
Number of Years of Gains: 24
Number of Years of Losses: 8
Net Expense Ratio: 0.76%
Category Average Net Expense Ratio: 1. 28 %
Open to all investors

**TOTAL ASSETS:** $1.24 billion

**NET ASSET ALLOCATION:**
Cash: 2.72%
Stock: 96.56%
Bonds: 0.00%
Other: 0.54%
Preferred: 0.72%

### FIVE YEAR RETURNS:

Year: 2018
Net Asset Value: $87.70   -2.44%
Distribution: $11.33   12.60%
Total Return: 10.17%

Year: 2017

Net Asset Value: $89.89   8.94%
Distribution: $12.06   14.62%
Total Return: 23.56%

Year: 2016
Net Asset Value: $82.51   -2.26%
Distribution: $3.81   4.51%
Total Return: 2.25%

Year: 2015
Net Asset Value: $84.42   2.80%
Distribution: $3.43   4.18%
Total Return: 6.98%

Year: 2014
Net Asset Value: $82.12   12.57%
Distribution: $7.45   10.21%
Total Return: 22.78%

**ANNUAL AVERAGE RETURNS:**

5-year average distribution: 9.22%
5-year average performance: 3.92%
5-year average return: 13.15%

3-year average distribution: 10.58%

3-year average performance: 1.42%
3-year average return: 11.99%

2-year average distribution: 13.61%
2-year average performance: 3.25%
2-year average return: 16.86%

There are 75 mutual funds in this category:

| As of: 3/15/19 | Fund Return | Category Average | Category *Rank |
|---|---|---|---|
| Year-to-date | 0.87% | 7.74% | 99% |
| 1-year | 8.01% | 6.32% | 48% |
| 3-year annualized | 13.92% | 15.41% | 62% |
| 5-year annualized | 12.76% | 9.75% | 22% |

Source: Wall Street Journal                    *1% Best – 100% Worst

Before making an investment, always read the mutual fund prospective.

Investment Fund Category:
**High Yield Municipal Debt Funds**

The Fund's objective is high level of interest income exempt from federal income tax that is consistent with the fund investment policies. Invest primarily in a portfolio of medium and low−grade municipal securities.

As the December 31, 2018, the average return for this category is 1.72%. This mutual fund's return is 4.61% compared to 189 total mutual funds.

**Goldman Sachs High Yield Muni A (GHYAX)**
800-526-7384
www.gsamfunds.com

Goldman Sachs Trust
71 South Wacker Drive - Suite 500
Chicago, IL 60606

Risk: above average
Minimum Investment Purchase: $1000

Minimum IRA Purchase: $250
Maximum Front End Sales Load: 4.50%
Date of Inception: April 3, 2000
Number of Years of Gains: 15
Number of Years of Losses: 3
Net Expense Ratio: 0.85%
Category Average Net Expense Ratio: 0.94%
Open to all investors

**TOTAL ASSETS:** $6.22 billion

**NET ASSET ALLOCATION:**
Cash: 1.22%
Stocks: 0%
Bonds: 98.38%
Other: 0.40%

### FIVE YEAR ANNUAL RETURNS:

Year: 2018
Net Asset Value: $9.62   0.73%
Distribution: $.37   3.88%
Total Return: 4.61%

Year: 2017
Net Asset Value: $9.55   4.60%

Distribution: $.39   4.27%
Return: 8.87%

Year: 2016
Net Asset Value: $9.13   –1.30%
Distribution: $.41   4.44%
Total Return: 3.14%

Year: 2015
Net Asset Value: $9.25   –0.96%
Distribution: $.43   4.60%
Total Return: 3.64%

Year: 2014
Net Asset Value: $9.34   10.14%
Distribution: $.42   4.95%
Total Return: 15.09%

## ANNUAL AVERAGE RETURNS:

5-year average distribution: 4.43%
5-year average performance: 2.64%
5-year average return: 7.07%

3-year average distribution: 4.19%
3-year average performance: 1.35%

3-year average return: 5.54%

2-year average distribution: 4.07%
2-year average performance: 2.67%
2-year average return: 6.74%

There are 189 mutual funds in this category:

| As of: 3/15/19 | Fund Return | Category Average | Category *Rank |
|---|---|---|---|
| Year-to-date | 2.54% | 2.11% | 15% |
| 1-year | 7.37% | 4.73% | 5% |
| 3-year annualized | 5.95% | 3.70% | 4% |
| 5-year annualized | 6.21% | 5.05% | 12% |

Source: Wall Street Journal          *1% Best – 100% Worst

Before making an investment, always read the mutual fund prospective.

Investment Fund Category:
**Intermediate Municipal Debt Funds**

The Fund's objective is high level of interest income exempt from federal income tax that is consistent with the fund investment policies. The fund invests primarily in a portfolio of medium and low–grade municipal securities.

As the December 31, 2018, the average return for this category is 0.72%. This mutual fund's return is 2.81% compared to 189 total mutual funds.

**Goldman Sachs Muni Income Fund  GSMIX)**
800-526-7384
www.gsamfunds.com

Goldman Sachs Trust
71 South Wacker Drive - Suite 500
Chicago, IL 60606

Risk: above average
Minimum Investment Purchase: $1000

Minimum IRA Purchase: $250
Maximum Front End Sales Load: 3.75%
Date of Inception: July 20, 1993
Number of Years of Gains: 20
Number of Years of Losses: 5
Net Expense Ratio: 0.76
Category Average Net Expense Ratio: 0.76
Open to all investors

**TOTAL ASSETS:** $3.29 billion

**NET ASSET ALLOCATION:**
Cash: 1.72%
Stock: 0.00%
Bonds: 97.89%
Other: 0.39%

### FIVE YEAR RETURNS:

Year: 2018
Net Asset Value: $15.67   0.00%
Distribution: $.44   2.81%
Total Return: 2.81%

Year: 2017
Net Asset Value: $15.67   2.42%

Distribution: $.47   3.07%
Total Return: 5.49%


Year: 2016
Net Asset Value: $15.30   -2.17%
Distribution: $.51   3.26%
Total Return: 1.09%


Year: 2015
Net Asset Value: $15.64   -1.76%
Distribution: $.54   3.39%
Total Return: 1.63%


Year: 2014
Net Asset Value: $15.92   6.28%
Distribution: $.56   3.74%
Total Return: 10.02%


## ANNUAL AVERAGE RETURNS:

5-year average distribution: 3.25%
5-year average performance: 0.95%
5-year average return: 4.21%

3-year average distribution: 3.05%
3-year average performance: 0.08%

3-year average return: 3.13%

2-year average distribution: 2.94%
2-year average performance: 1.21%
2-year average return: 4.15%

There are 78 mutual funds in this category:

| As of: 3/15/19 | Fund Return | Category Average | Category *Rank |
|---|---|---|---|
| Year-to-date | 2.02% | 1.75% | 14% |
| 1-year | 5.23% | 3.72% | 4% |
| 3-year annualized | 3.61% | 1.92% | 3% |
| 5-year annualized | 3.80% | 2.48% | 6% |

Source: Wall Street Journal          *1% Best – 100% Worst

Before making an investment, always read the mutual fund prospective.

## Investment Fund Category:
### Large-Cap Core

Large-Cap is an abbreviation of the term "large market capitalization". The market capitalization value is more than $10 billion. Fund's objective is to invest 80% of its net assets in common stocks of U.S. companies having large market capitalization, over $2 billion. The fund may also invest 20% of its assets in foreign securities.

As the December 31, 2018, the average return performance for this category is 5.65%. This mutual fund's return is 6.51% compared to 785 total mutual funds.

**American Century Focused Dynamic Growth Fund (ACFOX)**
800-345-2021
www.americancentury.com

American Century Growth Funds, Inc.
4500 Main Street, 9th Floor
Kansas City MO 64111

Risk: average
Minimum Investment Purchase: $2500
Minimum IRA Purchase: $2500
Maximum Front End Sales Load: No Load
Date of Inception: May 31, 2006
Number of Years of Gains: 10
Number of Years of Losses: 2
Net Expense Ratio: 0.85%
Category Average Net Expense Ratio: 1.10%
Open to all investors

**TOTAL ASSETS**: $110.13 million

**NET ASSET ALLOCATION:**
Cash: 3.92%
Stocks: 96.08%
Bonds: 0.00%

### FIVE YEAR RETURNS:

Year: 2018
Net Asset Value: $23.56   6.51%
Distribution: 0.00%
Total Return: 6.51%

Year: 2017

Net Asset Value: $22.12   34.55%
Distribution: 0.00%
Total Return: 34.55%

Year: 2016
Net Asset Value: $16.44   4.51%
Distribution: $.19   1.21%
Total Return: 5.14%

Year: 2015
Net Asset Value: $15.73   -4.84%
Distribution: $.21   1.27%
Total Return: -3.57%

Year: 2014
Net Asset Value $16.53   10.35%
Distribution: $.22   1.47%
Total Return: 11.82%

## ANNUAL AVERAGE RETURNS:

5-year average distribution: 0.79%
5-year average performance: 10.22%
5-year average return: 11.01%

3-year average distribution: 0.40%

3-year average performance: 15.19%
3-year average return: 15.59%

2-year average distribution: 0.00%
2-year average performance: 20.53%
2-year average return: 20.53%

There are 785 mutual funds in this category:

| As of: 3/15/19 | Fund Return | Category Average | Category *Rank |
|---|---|---|---|
| Year-to-date | 18.29% | 12.56% | 2% |
| 1-year | 12.88% | 3.45% | 1% |
| 3-year annualized | 22.61% | 12.89% | 1% |
| 5-year annualized | 13.82% | 9.54% | 1% |

Source: Wall Street Journal          *1% Best – 100% Worst

Before making an investment, always read the mutual fund prospective.

Investment Fund Category:
**Large-Cap Growth**

Large-Cap is an abbreviation of the term "large market capitalization". The market capitalization value is more than $10 billion. Funds objective is long-term growth by investing in stocks. The fund will usually invest 80% of its net assets in the common stocks of the diversified group of growth companies.

As the December 31, 2018 , the average return for this category is -0.80% This mutual fund's return is 1.82% compared to 693 total mutual funds.

**Edgewood Growth Fund Retail (EGFFX)**
800 791-4226
www.edgewoodfunds.com

Advisors' Inner Circle (Edgewood Growth)
P. O. Box 219009
Kansas City, MO 64121-9009

Risk: above average

Minimum Investment Purchase: $3000

Minimum IRA Purchase: $2000

Maximum Front End Sales Load: No Load

Date of Inception: February 28, 2006

Number of Years of Gains: 11

Number of Years of Losses: 1

Net Expense Ratio: 1.40%

Category Average Net Expense Ratio: 1.11%

Open to all investors

**TOTAL ASSETS:** $11.88 billion

**NET ASSET ALLOCATION:**
Cash: 1.96%

Stocks: 98.04%

Bonds: 0.00%

### FIVE YEAR RETURNS:

Year: 2018
Net Asset Value: $27.59   -3.19%
Distribution: $1.43   5.02%
Total Return: 1.83%

Year: 2017
Net Asset Value: $28.50   32.50%

Distribution: $.38   1.77%
Total Return: 34.27%


Year: 2016
Net Asset Value: $21.51    0.94%
Distribution: $.48   2.25%
Total Return: 3.19%


Year: 2015
Net Asset Value: $21.31    7.52%
Distribution: $.71   3.58%
Total Return: 11.10%


Year: 2014
Net Asset Value: $19.82   7.66%
Distribution: $1.00   5.43%
Total Return: 13.09%

**ANNUAL AVERAGE RETURNS:**

5-year average distribution: 3.61%
5-year average performance: 9.08%
5-year average return: 12.69%

3-year average distribution: 3.01%
3-year average performance: 10.08%

3-year average return: 13.09%

2-year average distribution: 3.39%
2-year average performance: 14.65%
2-year average return: 18.04%

There are 693 mutual funds in this category:

| As of: 3/15/19 | Fund Return | Category Average | Category *Rank |
|---|---|---|---|
| Year-to-date | 15.01% | 15.24% | 63% |
| 1-year | 4.80% | 5.49% | 59% |
| 3-year annualized | 20.34% | 16.79% | 6% |
| 5-year annualized | 15.10% | 11.83% | 3% |

Source: Wall Street Journal                     *1% Best – 100% Worst

Before making an investment, always read the mutual fund prospective.

Investment Fund Category:
**Large-Cap Value**

Large-Cap is an abbreviation of the term "large market capitalization". The market capitalization value is more than $10 billion. Funds objective is to invest in "undervalued" common stocks to provide long-term capital appreciation.

As the December 31, 2018, the average return for this category is -8.53%. This mutual fund's return is 2.80 compared to 479 total mutual funds.

**AMG Yacktman Focused Fund N  (YACKX)**
**800 835-3879**
www.amgfunds.com

AMG Funds
600 Steamboat Road, Suite 300
Greenwich, Connecticut 06830

Risk: below average

Minimum Investment Purchase: $2000
Minimum IRA Purchase: $1000
Maximum Front End Sales Load: No Load
Date of Inception: May 1, 1997
Number of Years of Gains: 17
Number of Years of Losses: 4
Net Expense Ratio: 1.00%
Category Average Net Expense Ratio: 0.88%

**TOTAL ASSETS:** $3.7 billion

**NET ASSET ALLOCATION:**
Cash: 28.42%
Stocks: 70.3%
Bonds: 1.28%
Other: 0.00%

### FIVE YEAR RETURNS:

Year: 2018
Net Asset Value: $17.78   –15.85%
Distribution: $3.94   18.65%
Total Return: 2.80%

Year: 2017
Net Asset Value: $21.13   7.31%

Distribution: $2.50   12.70%
Total Return: 20.01%


Year: 2016
Net Asset Value: $19.69   -0.40%
Distribution: $2.32   11.73%
Total Return: 11.33%


Year: 2015
Net Asset Value: $19.77   -23.61%
Distribution: $5.08   19.63%
Total Return: -3.98%


Year: 2014
Net Asset Value: $25.88   2.90%
Distribution: $1.98   7.87%
Total Return: 10.78%


ANNUAL AVERAGE RETURNS:


5-year average distribution: 14.12%
5-year average performance: -5.93%
5-year average return: 8.19%


3-year average distribution: 14.36%
3-year average performance: -2.98%

3-year average return: 11.38%

2–year average distribution: 15.67%
2-year average performance: -4.27%
2-year average return: 11.40%

There are 479 mutual funds in this category:

| As of: 3/15/19 | Fund Return | Category Average | Category *Rank |
|---|---|---|---|
| Year-to-date | 7.14% | 12.00% | 100% |
| 1-year | 8.88% | 1.98% | 4% |
| 3-year annualized | 12.31% | 11.10% | 21% |
| 5-year annualized | 9.04% | 7.72% | 13% |

Before making an investment, always read the mutual fund prospective.

# Investment Fund Category:
## MID-CAP CORE

Mid-Cap is an abbreviation of the term "mid-market capitalization" and has a market capitalization value of $1 billion to $8 billion. Mid-Cap funds are generally the most popular choice for investors seeking a fund with greater return possibilities with lower risks. Funds objective is long-term capital growth primarily in mid and small size companies.

As the December 31, 2018, the average return for this category is -11.77%. This mutual fund's return is -7.31% compared to 434 total mutual funds.

**Meridian Contrarian Legacy (MVALX)**
800 446-6662
www.meridianfund.com

Meridian Fund Inc.
60 E Sir Francis Drake Blvd, Suite 306
Larkspur CA 94939

Risk: Average
Minimum Investment Purchase: $1000
Minimum IRA Purchase: $1000
Maximum Front End Sales Load: no load
Date of Inception: February 10, 1994
Number of Years of Gains: 19
Number of Years of Losses: 5
Net Expense Ratio: 1.13%
Category Average Net Expense Ratio: 1.20%
Open to all investors

**TOTAL ASSETS:** $547.25 million

**NET ASSET ALLOCATION:**
Cash: 6.84%
Stocks: 93.16%
Bonds: 0.00%
Other: 0.00%

### FIVE YEAR RETURNS:

Year: 2018
Net Asset Value: $30.90   -26.36%
Distribution: $7.99   19.05%
Total Return: -7.31%

Year: 2017
Net Asset Value: $41.96   12.83%
Distribution: $4.46  11.99%
Total Return: 24.82%

Year: 2016
Net Asset Value: $37.19   16.00%
Distribution: $.19   0.59%
Total Return: 16.59%

Year: 2015
Net Asset Value: $32.06   –17.35%
Distribution: $5.37   13.84%
Total Return: –3.51%

Year: 2014
Net Asset Value: $38.79   –11.74%
Distribution: $7.88  17.94%
Total Return: 6.20%

## ANNUAL AVERAGE RETURNS:

5-year average distribution: 12.68%
5-year average performance: –5.32%
5-year average return: 7.36%

3-year average distribution: 10.55%
3-year average performance: 0.82%
3-year average return: 11.37%

2-year average distribution: 15.52%
2-year average performance: -6.77%
2-year average return: 8.76%

There are 434 mutual funds in this category:

| As of: 3/15/19 | Fund Return | Category Average | Category *Rank |
|---|---|---|---|
| Year-to-date | 15.57% | 14.12% | 21% |
| 1-year | 1.46% | -0.21% | 26% |
| 3-year annualized | 17.19% | 10.67% | 2% |
| 5-year annualized | 9.95% | 6.39% | 5% |

Source: Wall Street Journal          *1% Best – 100% Worst

Before making an investment, always read the mutual fund prospective.

Investment Fund Category:
**Mid-Cap Growth**

Mid-Cap is the term for "mid-market capitalization" and has a market capitalization value of $1 billion to $8 billion. Mid-Cap mutual funds are generally the most popular choice for investors seeking a fund with greater return possibilities with lower risks. The funds objective is capital appreciation by investing 80% of the assets in this market.

As the December 31, 2018, the average return for this category was -5.35%. This mutual fund's return was 4.69% compared to 393 total mutual funds.

**Value Line Mid-Cap Focused Fund (VLIFX)**
800-243-2729
www.vlfunds.com

Value Line Income & Growth Fund, Inc.
220 E. 42nd St.
New York, New York 10017

Risk: low
Minimum Investment Purchase: $1000
Minimum IRA Purchase: $1000
Maximum Front End Sales Load: No Load
Date of Inception: March 1, 1950
Number of Years of Gains: 53
Number of Years of Losses: 15
Net Expense Ratio: 1.18%
Category Average Net Expense Ratio: 1.20%
Open to all investors

**TOTAL ASSETS:** $186.2 million

**NET ASSET ALLOCATION:**
Cash: 1.70%
Stocks: 98.30%
Bonds: 0.00%

### FIVE YEAR RETURNS:

Year: 2018
Net Asset Value: $19.11   -0.42%
Distribution: $.98   5.11%
Total Return: 4.69%

Year: 2017
Net Asset Value: $19.19   17.95%

Distribution: $0.00    0.00%
Total Return: 17.95%

Year: 2016
Net Asset Value: $16.27    8.54%
Distribution: $.36    2.40%
Total Return: 10.94%

Year: 2015
Net Asset Value: $14.99    2.95%
Distribution: $6.85    3.66%
Total Return: 6.61%

Year: 2014
Net Asset Value: $14.56    7.85%
Distribution: $.01    0.07%
Total Return: 7.92%

## ANNUAL AVERAGE RETURNS:

5-year average distribution: 2.25%
5-year average performance: 7.37%
5-year average return: 9.62%

3-year average distribution: 2.50%
3-year average performance: 8.69%

3-year average return: 11.19%

2-year average distribution: 2.56%
2-year average performance: 8.77%
2-year average return: 11.33%

There are 393 mutual funds in this category:

| As of: 3/15/19 | Fund Return | Category Average | Category *Rank |
|---|---|---|---|
| Year-to-date | 14.97% | 18.15% | 91% |
| 1-year | 14.83% | 5.36% | 5% |
| 3-year annualized | 17.32% | 16.06% | 30% |
| 5-year annualized | 11.93% | 9.18% | 10% |

Source: Wall Street Journal                    *1% Best – 100% Worst

Before making an investment, always read the mutual fund prospective.

## Investment Fund Category:
## **Mixed–Asset Target Allocation:**
## **Conservative**

Fund's objective is to provide long-term growth and high level of income. Usually the conservative fund invests 40% in stocks, 40% in bonds and 15% in cash.

As the December 31, 2018, the average return for this category was -4.12%. This mutual fund's return was -2.49% compared to 353 total mutual funds.

**Vanguard Wellesley Income  (VWINX)**
800-662-7447
www.vanguard.com

Vanguard Group
P. O. Box 2600 – V 26
Valley Forge PA 19482

Risk: below average
Minimum Investment Purchase: $3000

Minimum IRA Purchase: $3000
Maximum Front End Sales Load: No Load
Date of Inception: July 1, 1970
Number of Years of Gains: 41
Number of Years of Losses: 7
Net Expense Ratio: 0.23%
Category Average Net Expense Ratio: 79%
Open to all investors

**TOTAL ASSETS**: $50.23 billion

**NET ASSET ALLOCATION:**
Cash: 1.41%
Stocks: 36.74%
Bonds: 59.77% %
Other: 1.93%
Convertible: 0.15%

### FIVE YEAR RETURNS:

Year: 2018
Net Asset Value: $24.43   −9.35%
Distribution: $1.85   6.86%
Total Return:   −2.49%

Year: 2017

Net Asset Value: $26.95   5.81%
Distribution: $1.12   4.39%
Total Return: 10.20%


Year: 2016
Net Asset Value: $25.47   3.87%
Distribution: $1.03   4.21%
Total Return: 8.08%


Year: 2015
Net Asset Value: $24.52   -4.11%
Distribution: $1.38   5.40%
Total Return: 1.29%


Year: 2014
Net Asset Value: $25.57   2.90%
Distribution: $1.28   5.17%
Total Return: 8.07%


## ANNUAL AVERAGE RETURNS:

5-year average distribution: 5.21%
5-year average performance: 0.18%
5-year average return: 5.39%

3-year average distribution: 5.15%

3-year average performance: 0.11%
3-year average return: 5.26%

2-year average distribution: 5.63%
2-year average performance: -1.77%
2-year average return: 3.86%

There are 353 mutual funds in this category:

| As of: 3/15/19 | Fund Return | Category Average | Category *Rank |
|---|---|---|---|
| Year-to-date | 5.94% | 5.63% | 41% |
| 1-year | 5.25% | 1.64% | 5% |
| 3-year annualized | 6.39% | 5.18% | 16% |
| 5-year annualized | 5.86% | 3.40% | 3% |

Source: Wall Street Journal          *1% Best – 100% Worst

Before making an investment, always read the mutual fund prospective.

Investment Fund Category:
**Mixed–Asset Target Allocation Growth**

Fund's objective is to provide long-term growth and high level of income. Usually a moderate fund invests 65% in stocks, 30% in bonds and 5% in cash.

As the December 31, 2018, the average return for this category was -6.80%. This mutual fund's return was -2.71% compared to 500 total mutual funds.

**Value Line Income & Growth   (VALIX)**
800-243-2729
www.vlfunds.com

Value Line Income & Growth Fund, Inc.
220 E. 42nd St.
New York, New York 10017

Risk: above average
Minimum Investment Purchase: $1000
Minimum IRA Purchase: $1000

Maximum Front End Sales Load: No Load
Date of Inception: August 24, 199
Number of Years of Gains: 22
Number of Years of Losses: 3
Net Expense Ratio: 1.12%
Category Average Net Expense Ratio: 0.84%
Open to all investors

**TOTAL ASSETS**: $387.69 million

**NET ASSET ALLOCATION**:
Cash: 2.89%
Stocks: 69.28% %
Bond: 27.71%
Other: 0.12%

### FIVE YEAR RETURNS:

Year: 2018
Net Asset Value: $8.94   –10.15%
Dividend Distribution:  $.74   7.44%
Total Return:  –2.71%

Year: 2017
Net Asset Value: $9.95   17.33%
Dividend Distribution: $.55   6.53%

Total Return: 23.86%


Year: 2016
Net Asset Value: $8.48  -2.75%
Dividend Distribution: $.48  5.54%
Total Return: 2.79%


Year: 2015
Net Asset Value: $8.72  -7.23%
Dividend Distribution: $.60  6.38%
Total Return: -0.85%


Year: 2014
Net Asset Value: $9.40  -4.28%
Dividend Distribution $1.46  14.88%
Total Return: 10.60%

## ANNUAL AVERAGE RETURNS:

5-year average distribution: 8.16%
5-year average performance: -1.42%
5-year average return: 6.74%


3-year average distribution: 6.50%
3-year average performance: 1.48%
3-year average return: 7.98%

2-year average distribution: 6.99%

2-year average performance: 3.59%

2-year average return: 10.58%

There are 500 mutual funds in this category:

| As of: 3/15/19 | Fund Return | Category Average | Category *Rank |
|---|---|---|---|
| Year-to-date | 17.23% | 9.55% | 1% |
| 1-year | 5.95% | 0.82% | 3% |
| 3-year annualized | 14.89% | 8.74% | 1% |
| 5-year annualized | 9.57% | 5.78% | 2% |

Source: Wall Street Journal                    *1% Best – 100% Worst

Before making an investment, always read the mutual fund prospective.

## Investment Fund Category
## **Mixed—Asset Target Allocation: Moderate**

Fund's objective is to provide long-term growth and high level of income. Usually the growth fund invests 80% in stocks, 15% in bonds and 5% in cash.

As the December 31, 2018, the average return for this category was -5.76%. This mutual fund's return was 0.58% compared to the total mutual funds.

**Janus Henderson Balanced T (JABAX)**
877-335-2687
www.janushenderson.com

Janus Investment Fund
151 Detroit Street
Denver CO 80206

Risk: average
Minimum Investment Purchase: $2500
Minimum IRA Purchase: $2500

Maximum Front End Sales Load: no load
Date of Inception: September 1, 1992
Number of Years of Gains: 22
Number of Years of Losses: 4
Net Expense Ratio: 0.82%
Category Average Net Expense Ratio: 0.84%
Open to all investors
**TOTAL ASSETS:** $15.67 billion

**NET ASSET ALLOCATION**:

Cash: 0.79%
Stocks: 61.05%
Bonds: 37.78%
Other: 0.38%

## FIVE YEAR RETURNS:

Year: 2018
Net Asset Value: $30.93   -5.96%
Distribution: $2.15   6.54%
Total Return: 0.58%

Year: 2017
Net Asset Value: $32.89   12.44%
Distribution: $1.71   5.85%

Total Return: 18.29%

Year: 2016
Net Asset Value: $29.25   1.07%
Distribution: $.96   3.32%
Total Return: 4.39%

Year: 2015
Net Asset Value: $28.94   -5.36%
Distribution: $1.79   5.85%
Total Return: 0.49%

Year: 2014
Net Asset Value: $30.58   2.00%
Dividend Distribution: $1.87   6.24%
Total Return: 8.24%

## ANNUAL AVERAGE RETURNS:

5-year average distribution: 5.56%
5-year average performance: 0.84%
5-year average return: 6.40%

3-year average distribution: 5.23%
3-year average performance: 2.52%
3-year average return: 7.75%

2-year average distribution: 6.19%
2-year average performance: 3.24%
2-year average return: 9.43%

There are 600 mutual funds in this category:

| As of: 3/15/19 | Fund Return | Category Average | Category *Rank |
|---|---|---|---|
| Year-to-date | 8.05% | 7.81% | 43% |
| 1-year | 6.32% | 1.26% | 2% |
| 3-year annualized | 11.32% | 7.20% | 2% |
| 5-year annualized | 7.71% | 4.63% | 2% |

Source: Wall Street Journal                    *1% Best – 100% Worst

Before making an investment, always read the mutual fund prospective.

# Investment Fund Category:
## Multi-Cap Growth

Multi-cap is a diversified market which invests in stocks across market capitalization. Portfolio includes large-cap, mid-cap, and small-cap. Usually multi-caps are less risky compared to pure mid-cap or small-cap and is less aggressive. Fund's objective is to increase the value of the investment over the long-term. The fund primarily invests in domestic common stocks of a variety size companies.

As the December 31, 2018, the average return for this category was -2.95%. This mutual fund's return was 3.63% compared to 571 total mutual funds.

**Federated Kaufmann A  (KAUAX)**
800-341-7400
www.federatedinvestors.com

Federated Kaufmann A
Federated Investors Tower
Pittsburgh, PA 15222−3779

Risk: above average
Minimum Investment Purchase: $1500
Minimum IRA Purchase: $250
Maximum Front End Sales Load: 5.50%
Date of Inception: April 24, 2001
Number of Years of Gains: 14
Number of Years of Losses: 3
Net Expense Ratio: 1.95%
Category Average Net Expense Ratio: 1.20%
Open to all investors

**TOTAL ASSETS:** $5.53 billion

**NET ASSET ALLOCATION:**
Cash: 18.91%
Stocks: 80.94%
Bonds: 0.00%
Other: 0.15%

## FIVE YEAR RETURNS:

Year: 2018
Net Asset Value: $5.06   -9.48%
Dividend Distribution: $.73   13.11%
Total Return: 3.63%

Year: 2017

Net Asset Value: $5.59   13.85%
Dividend Distribution: $.68   13.85%
Total Return: 27.70%

Year: 2016
Net Asset Value: $4.91   –6.65%
Dividend Distribution: $.52   9.89%
Total Return: 3.23%

Year: 2015
Net Asset Value: $5.26   –8.84%
Dividend Distribution: $.86   14.90%
Total Return: 6.06% %

Year: 2014
Net Asset Value: $5.77   –6.33%
Dividend Distribution: $.86   13.96%
Total Return: 7.63%

## ANNUAL AVERAGE RETURNS:

5-year average distribution: 13.14%
5-year average performance: –3.49%
5-year average return: 9.65%

3-year average distribution: 12.28%

3-year average performance: -0.76%
3-year average return: 11.52%

2-year average distribution: 13.48%
2-year average performance: 2.19%
2-year average return: 15.67%

## There are 571 mutual funds in this category:

| As of: 3/15/19 | Fund Return | Category Average | Category *Rank |
|---|---|---|---|
| Year-to-date | 19.25% | 18.15% | 27% |
| 1-year | 9.83% | 5.36% | 13% |
| 3-year annualized | 22.73% | 16.06% | 4% |
| 5-year annualized | 12.61% | 9.18% | 6% |

Source: Wall Street Journal          *1% Best – 100% Worst

Before making an investment, always read the mutual fund prospective.

## Investment Fund Category:
## Multi-Cap Value

Multi-cap is a diversified market, the portfolio includes large-cap, mid-cap, and small-cap. Usually multi-caps are less risky compared to pure mid-cap or small-cap and are less aggressive. Fund's objective is capital growth over the long-term and income secondarily. Invests in stocks of established companies selling below what RE Advisors believe to be the fundamental value.

As the December 31, 2018, the average return for this category was -11.46%. This mutual fund's return was 16.22% compared to 417 total mutual funds.

**Copley Fund (COPLX)**
877-881-2751

Copley Fund Inc.
5348 Vegas Drive
Las Vegas NV 89108

Risk: below average
Minimum Investment Purchase: $1000
Minimum IRA Purchase: $1000
Maximum Front End Sales Load: no load
Date of Inception: September 1, 1978
Number of Years of Gains: 31
Number of Years of Losses: 99
Net Expense Ratio: 1.55%
Category Average Net Expense Ratio: 1.06%
Open to all investors

**TOTAL ASSETS:** $89.45

**NET ASSET ALLOCATION**:
Cash: 2.42%
Stocks: 97.58%
Bonds: 0.00%

## FIVE YEAR RETURNS:

Year: 2018
Net Asset Value: $102.75   16.22%
Distribution: $0.00   0.00%
Total Return: 16.22%

Year: 2017
Net Asset Value: $88.41   9.68%

Distribution: $0.00   0.00%
Total Return: 9.68%


Year: 2016
Net Asset Value: $80.61   15.55%
Distribution: $0.00   0.00%
Total Return: 15.55%


Year: 2015
Net Asset Value: $69.76   -1.98%
Distribution: $0.00   0.00%
Total Return: -1.98%


Year: 2014
Net Asset Value: $71.17   14.24%
Distribution: $0.00   0.00%
Total Return: 14.24%

## ANNUAL AVERAGE RETURNS:

5-year average distribution: 0.00%
5-year average performance: 10.74%
5-year average return: 10.74%

3-year average distribution: 0.00%
3-year average performance: 13.82%

3-year average return: 13.82%

2-year average distribution: 0.00%
2-year average performance: 12.95%
2-year average return: 12.95%

## There are 417 mutual funds in this category:

| As of: 3/15/19 | Fund Return | Category Average | Category *Rank |
|---|---|---|---|
| Year-to-date | 9.67% | 12.76% | 96% |
| 1-year | 13.00% | -0.49% | 1% |
| 3-year annualized | 14.69% | 10.34% | 2% |
| 5-year annualized | 12.03% | 6.86% | 1% |

Source: Wall Street Journal            *1% Best – 100% Worst

Before making an investment, always read the mutual fund prospective

## Investment Fund Category:
### Small-Cap Core

Small-cap is a "small market capitalization". Small-cap companies include market capitalization of less than $1 billion. Usually the companies are smaller and are upstarts having growth potential, but are not as financially strong as established in large companies. Fund's objective is long-term capital growth. The fund invests in growth common stocks that conform to a quantitative formula (Cornerstone Growth Strategy®).

As the December 31, 2018, the average return for this category was -10.74%. This mutual fund's return was -2.19% compared to 998 total mutual funds.

**Paradigm Value (PVFAX)**
877-593-8637
www.paradigm-funds.com

Paradigm Funds Trust
Nine Elk Street
Albany, NY 12207

Risk: below average
Minimum Investment Purchase: $2500
Minimum IRA Purchase: $1000
Maximum Front End Sales Load: No Load
Date of Inception: December 31, 2002
Number of Years of Gains: 13
Number of Years of Losses: 3
Net Expense Ratio: 1.50%
Category Average Net Expense Ratio: 1.15%
Open to all investors

**TOTAL ASSETS:** $51.64 million

**NET ASSET ALLOCATION:**
Cash: 5.05%
Stocks: 94.95%
Bonds: 0.00%

## FIVE YEAR RETURNS:

Year: 2018
Net Asset Value: $41.94   −14.34%
Distribution: $5.95   12.15%
Total Return: −2.19%

Year: 2017

Net Asset Value: $48.96   1.79%
Distribution: $5.96   12.39%
Total Return: 14.18%

Year: 2016
Net Asset Value: $48.10   11.81%
Distribution: $2.36   5.49%
Total Return: 17.29%

Year: 2015
Net Asset Value: $43.02   -11.02%
Distribution: $6.03   12.47%
Total Return: -0.63%

Year: 2014
Net Asset Value: $48.35   -14.23%
Distribution: $9.49   16.84%
Total Return: 2.61%

## ANNUAL AVERAGE RETURNS:

5-year average distribution: 11.87%
5-year average performance: -5.20%
5-year average return: 6.67%

3-year average distribution: 10.01%

3-year average performance: -0.25%
3-year average return: 9.76%

2-year average distribution: 12.27%
2-year average performance: -6.28%
2-year average return: 6.00%

**There are 998 mutual funds in this category:**

| As of: 3/15/19 | Fund Return | Category Average | Category *Rank |
|---|---|---|---|
| Year-to-date | 11.80% | 14.38% | 91% |
| 1-year | 4.13% | -1.68% | 9% |
| 3-year annualized | 15.26% | 11.82% | 9% |
| 5-year annualized | 7.99% | 6.04% | 16% |

Source: Wall Street Journal          *1% Best – 100% Worst

Before making an investment, always read the mutual fund prospective.

## Investment Fund Category:
### Small-Cap Growth

Small-cap is an abbreviation of the term "small market capitalization". Small-cap companies include market capitalization of less than $1 billion. Usually the companies are smaller and are upstarts having growth potential, but are not as financially strong as established in large companies. Fund's objective is long-term capital appreciation. Fund invests mainly in stocks of small companies that have growth potential. These companies usually provide little or no dividend income.

As the December 31, 2018, the average return for this category was -4.52%. This mutual fund's return was 10.28% compared to 578 total mutual funds.

**Wasatch Ultra Growth (WAMCX)**
800-551-1700
www.wasatchfunds.com

Wasatch Funds Trust
150 Social Hall Ave. – 4<sup>th</sup> floor
Salt Lake City, UT 84111

Risk: above average
Minimum Investment Purchase: $2000
Minimum IRA Purchase: $2000
Maximum Front End Sales Load: No Load
Date of Inception: August 17, 1992
Number of Years of Gains: 20
Number of Years of Losses: 6
Net Expense Ratio: 1.24%
Category Average Net Expense Ratio: 1.22%
Open to all investors

**TOTAL ASSETS:** $254.73 million

**NET ASSET ALLOCATION**:
Cash: 10.03%
Stocks: 87.92%
Bonds: 0.00%
Other: 2.05%

**FIVE YEAR RETURNS:**

Year: 2018

Net Asset Value: $21.01   2.44%
Distribution: $1.61   7.84%
Total Return: 10.28%


Year: 2017
Net Asset Value: $20.51   17.60%
Distribution: $2.44   13.99%
Total Return: 31.59%


Year: 2016
Net Asset Value: $17.44   -3.00%
Distribution: $2.00  11.12%
Total Return: 8.12%


Year: 2015
Net Asset Value: $17.98   -5.67%
Distribution: $1.65   8.66%
Total Return: 2.99%


Year: 2014
Net Asset Value: $19.06   -24.12%
Distribution: $6.89   27.43%
Total Return: 3.31%


**ANNUAL AVERAGE RETURNS:**

5-year average distribution: 13.81%
5-year average performance: -2.55%
5-year average return: 11.26%

3-year average distribution: 10.98%
3-year average performance: 5.68%
3-year average return: 16.66%

2-year average distribution: 10.92%
2-year average performance: 10.02%
2-year average return: 20.94%

**There are 578 mutual funds in this category:**

| As of: 3/15/19 | Fund Return | Category Average | Category *Rank |
|---|---|---|---|
| Year-to-date | 20.18% | 18.66% | 32% |
| 1-year | 19.69% | 6.30% | 5% |
| 3-year annualized | 29.07% | 18.75% | 3% |
| 5-year annualized | 14.17% | 8.51% | 3% |

Source: Wall Street Journal                    *1% Best – 100% Worst

Before making an investment, always read the mutual fund prospective.

Investment Fund Category:
**Small-Cap Value**

Small-cap is a "small market capitalization". Small-cap companies include market capitalization of less than $1 billion. Usually the companies are smaller and are upstarts having growth potential, but are not as financially strong as established in large companies. Fund's objective is long – term capital appreciation. 80% of the fund's net assets are invested in equity securities of small-cap companies that are within the range of the market capitalization of companies in the Russell 2000 Value Index. These companies pay little or no dividends.

As the December 31, 2018, the average return for this category was -16.04%. This mutual fund's return was -5.43% compared to 308 total mutual funds.

**Longleaf Partners Small-Cap (LLSCX)**

800-445-9469

www.longleafpartners.com

Longleaf Partners Funds Trust
6410 Poplar Ave, Suite 900
Memphis, TN 38119

Risk: below average
Minimum Investment Purchase: $10,000
Minimum IRA Purchase: $10,000
Maximum Front End Sales Load: no load
Date of Inception: February 21, 1989
Number of Years of Gains: 24
Number of Years of Losses: 5
Net Expense Ratio: 0.92%
Category Average Net Expense Ratio: 1.07%
Open to all investors

**TOTAL ASSETS:** $3.12 billion

**NET ASSET ALLOCATION:**
Cash: 25.21%
Stocks: 70.12%
Bonds: 4.67%

**FIVE YEAR RETURNS:**

Year: 2018
Net Asset Value: $22.10   –19.93%
Distribution: $4.00   14.49%

Total Return: –5.43%


Year: 2017
Net Asset Value: $27.60   0.40%
Distribution: $2.32   8.44%
Total Return: 8.84%


Year: 2016
Net Asset Value: $27.49   28.16%
Distribution: $4.96   23.12%
Total Return: 51.28%


Year: 2015
Net Asset Value: $21.45   –29.49%
Distribution: $1.60   5.26%
Total Return: –24.23%


Year: 2014
Net Asset Value: $30.42   –6.28%
Distribution: $6.02   18.55%
Total Return: 12.27%


**ANNUAL AVERAGE RETURNS:**

5-year average distribution: 13.98%
5-year average performance: –5.43%

5-year average return: 8.55%

3-year average distribution: 15.35%
3-year average performance: 2.88%
3-year average return: 18.23%

2-year average distribution: 11.47%
2-year average performance: -9.76%
2-year average return: 1.71%

**There are 308 mutual funds in this category:**

| As of: 3/15/19 | Fund Return | Category Average | Category *Rank |
|---|---|---|---|
| Year-to-date | 11.99% | 13.89% | 90% |
| 1-year | 4.13% | -3.86% | 4% |
| 3-year annualized | 10.32% | 10.19% | 43% |
| 5-year annualized | 6.90% | 4.19% | 11% |

Source: Wall Street Journal          *1% Best – 100% Worst

Before making an investment, always read the mutual fund prospective.

Investment Fund Category:
**Telecommunication**

The Fund's objective is to provide long-term capital growth from the common stocks of media, technology, and telecommunication companies. The fund invests in companies with large capitalization to mid-capitalization range.

As of December 31, 2018, the average return for this category was -8.46%. This mutual fund's return was -1.83% compared to 37 total mutual funds.

**Price Media & Telecom (PRMTX)**
800-638-5660
www.troweprice.com

T. Rowe Price Funds
100 East Pratt St.
Baltimore, MD 21202

Risk: high

Minimum Investment Purchase: $2500
Minimum IRA Purchase: $1000
Maximum Front End Sales Load: None
Date of Inception: October 13, 1993
Number of Years of Gains: 18
Number of Years of Losses: 7
Net Expense Ratio: 0.78%
Category Average Net Expense Ratio: 1.40%
Open to all investors

**TOTAL ASSETS:** $4.75 million

**NET ASSET ALLOCATION:**
Cash: 1.05%
Stocks: 98.95%
Bonds: 0.00%

### FIVE YEAR RETURNS:

Year: 2018
Net Asset Value: $93.56   -3.02%
Distribution: $1.15   1.19%
Total Return: -1.83%

Year: 2017
Net Asset Value: $96.47   29.93%

Distribution: $2.28   3.06%
Total Return: 32.99%


Year: 2016
Net Asset Value: $74.25   5.16%
Distribution: $1.65   2.33%
Total Return: 7.49%


Year: 2015
Net Asset Value $70.61   8.51%
Distribution: $2.26   3.48%
Total Return: 11.99%


Year: 2014
Net Asset Value: $65.07    −6.32%
Distribution: $7.27   10.46%
Total Return: 4.14%


## ANNUAL AVERAGE RETURNS:

5-year average distribution: 4.11%
5-year average performance: 6.85%
5-year average return: 10.96%

3-year average distribution: 2.19%
3-year average performance: 10.69%

3-year average return: 12.88%

2-year average distribution: 2.13%
2-year average performance: 13.45%
2-year average return: 15.58%

**There are 37 mutual funds in this category:**

| As of: 3/15/19 | Fund Return | Category Average | Category *Rank |
|---|---|---|---|
| Year-to-date | 18.11% | 12.51% | 9% |
| 1-year | 5.00% | 1.91% | 16% |
| 3-year annualized | 20.07% | 6.88% | 4% |
| 5-year annualized | 13.98% | 5.49% | 4% |

Source: Wall Street Journal                     *1% Best – 100% Worst

Before making an investment, always read the mutual fund prospective.

Investment Fund Category:
**U. S. Mortgage Fund**

The Fund's objective seeks high total return. At least of 80% of its assets is invested in mortgage backed securities and other mortgage related securities issued or guaranteed by the U.S. Government or various U.S. Government agencies.

As the December 31, 2018, the average return for this category was 0.75%. This mutual fund's return is 1.48% compared to 124 total mutual funds.

**Columbia  Quality Income Fund A  (AUGAX)**
800–345–6611
www.columbisthreadneedleus.com

Columbia Management Investment Services
P.  O.  Box 8081
Boston, MA 02266 – 8081

Risk: low

Minimum Investment Purchase: $2000
Minimum IRA Purchase: $1000
Maximum Front End Sales Load: 4. 75%
Date of Inception: February 14, 2002
Number of Years of Gains: 14
Number of Years of Losses: 2
Net Expense Ratio: 0.91%
Category Average Net Expense Ratio: 0.76%
Open to all investors

**TOTAL ASSETS:** $1.79 billion

**NET ASSET ALLOCATION:**
Cash: 19.66%
Stocks: 0.00%
Bonds: 80.34%

### FIVE YEAR RETURNS:

Year: 2018
Net Asset Value:  $5.37   -0.92%
Distribution:  $.13   2.40%
Total Return:  1.48%

Year: 2017
Net Asset Value:  $5.42   0.37%

Distribution:  $.14   2.59%
Total Return:  2.96%


Year: 2016
Net Asset Value: $5.40   –0.37%
Distribution: $.14   2.58%
Total Return: 2.21%


Year: 2015
Net Asset Value: $5.42   –1.81%
Distribution: $.16   2.95%
Total Return: 1.14%


Year: 2014
Net Asset Value: $5.52   2.79%
Distribution: $.34   6.42%
Total Return: 9.21%


### ANNUAL AVERAGE RETURNS:

5-year average distribution: 3.39%
5-year average performance: 0.01%
5-year average return: 3.40%

3-year average distribution: 2.52%
3-year average performance: –0.31%

3-year average return: 2.22%

2-year average distribution: 2.50%
2-year average performance: -0.28%
2-year average return: 2.22%

**There are 124 mutual funds in this category:**

| As of: 3/15/19 | Fund Return | Category Average | Category *Rank |
|---|---|---|---|
| Year-to-date | 1.50% | 1.49% | 29% |
| 1-year | 4.29% | 3.55% | 17% |
| 3-year annualized | 2.44% | 2.01% | 25% |
| 5-year annualized | 2.63% | 2.16% | 24% |

Source: Wall Street Journal                    *1% Best − 100% Worst

Before making an investment, always read the mutual fund prospective.

Investment Fund Category:
**Utilities**

The funds objective is capital appreciation and current income. Usually 80% of its net assets are invested in securities of public utilities companies. These companies provide electricity, natural gas, water, and communications service to the public. The investments are in equity securities that are mainly of common stocks.

As the December 31, 2018, the average return for this category was 2.06%. This mutual fund's return is 9.01% compared to 64 total mutual funds.

**Fidelity Select Utilities (FSUTX)**
800-544-8544
www.institutional.fidelity.com

Fidelity Select Portfolios
82 Devonshire St.
Boston, MA 02109

Risk: average

Minimum Investment Purchase: $2500

Minimum IRA Purchase: $2500

Maximum Front End Sales Load: No Load

Date of Inception: December 9, 1981

Number of Years of Gains: 30

Number of Years of Losses: 7

Net Expense Ratio: 0.77%

Category Average Net Expense Ratio: 1.15%

Open to all investors

**TOTAL ASSETS**: $949.91 million

**NET ASSET ALLOCATION:**

Cash: 0.39%

Stocks: 99.61%

Bonds: 0.00%

### FIVE YEAR RETURNS:

Year: 2018

Net Asset Value: $80.12   0.44%

Distribution: $6.84   8.57%

Total Return: 9.01%

Year: 2017

Net Asset Value: $79.77   11.91%

Distribution: $4.48    6.28%
Total Return: 18.19%

Year: 2016
Net Asset Value: $71.28    11.10%
Distribution: $1.79    2.78%
Total Return: 13.88%

Year: 2015
Net Asset Value: $64.16    -14.61%
Distribution: $2.80    3.73%
Total Return: -10.89%

Year: 2014
Net Asset Value: $75.14    12.81%
Distribution: $1.28    1.92%
Total Return: 14.73%

## ANNUAL AVERAGE RETURNS:

5-year average distribution: 3.50%
5-year average performance: 7.76%
5-year average return: 11.26%

3-year average distribution:  5.88%
3-year average performance:  7.82%

3-year average return: 13.70%

2-year average distribution:  7.43%
2-year average performance:  6.17%
2-year average return:  13.60%

## There are 64 mutual funds in this category:

| As of: 3/15/19 | Fund Return | Category Average | Category *Rank |
|---|---|---|---|
| Year-to-date | 9.76% | 8.40% | 11% |
| 1-year | 19.07% | 17.86% | 40% |
| 3-year annualized | 13.69% | 10.60% | 2% |
| 5-year annualized | 10.02% | 8.13% | 5% |

Source: Wall Street Journal                    *1% Best – 100% Worst

Before making an investment, always read the mutual fund prospective.

FINANCIAL WEALTH

Here is an excellent model of how to build wealth for savings or retirement. This 9-year investment formula includes the mutual fund performance, distribution and reinvestment.

Mutual Fund: **Oakmark I (OAKMX)**
Investment Category: Large-Cap Core
Maximum Front End Sales Load: No Load

June 1, 2010
IRA purchase: $6000.
Net asset value (share price): $36.91
Total shares: 162.5576

December 17, 2010

Distribution:  $.25 x 162.5576 = $40.64.
Shares reinvested: 1.0098
Total shares owned: 163.5674

December 31, 2010
Net asset value: $41.30.
**IRA value: $6755.33 – 12.59% return**

June 1, 2011
IRA purchase: $6000
Net asset value: $43.74
Total shares: 137.1742

December 19, 2011
Distribution:  $.35 x 300.7416 = $105.26.
Shares reinvested: 2.6341
Total shares owned: 303.3757

December 30, 2011
Net asset value: $41.69.
**IRA value: $12,647.73 – 5. 40% return**

June 1, 2012
IRA purchase: $6000
Net asset value: $42.83
Total shares owned: 140.0887

December 18, 2012
Distribution $1.88 x 480.3828 = $903.12.
Shares reinvested: 19.3595
Total shares owned: 462.8239

December 31, 2012
Net asset value: $48.53.
**IRA value: $22,460.84 – 24.78% return**

June 1, 2013
IRA purchase: $6500
Net asset value: $57.16
Total shares owned: 113.7159

December 19, 2013
Distribution $2.92 x 576.5398 = $1683.50.
Shares reinvested:  27.1138
Total shares owned: 603.6536

December 31, 2013
Net asset value: $62.09
**IRA value: $37,480.85 – 52.98% return**

June 1, 2014
IRA purchase: $6500
Net asset value: $66.67
Total shares owned: 97.4951

December 18, 2014
Distribution $4.55 x 701.1487 = $3190.23.
Shares reinvested: 48.2636
Total shares owned: 749.4123

December 31, 2014
Net asset value $66.38
**IRA value: $49,745.99 – 60.47% return**

June 1, 2015
IRA purchase: $6500
Net asset value: $67.66
Total shares owned: 96.0686

December 17, 2015
Distribution $.90 x 845.4809 = $760.93.
Shares reinvested: 12.1148
Total shares owned: 857.5957

December 31, 2015
Net asset value: $62.86.
**IRA value: $53,908.47 – 43.76% return**

June 1, 2016
Max. IRA purchase:  $6500
Net asset value: $64.88
Total shares owned: 100.1850

November 28, 2016
Distribution $1.87 x 857.5957 = $1603.70.
Shares reinvested: 22.7250
Total shares owned: 980.5057

December 30, 2016
Net asset value $72.48
Total investment: $44,000
**IRA value: $71,067.05 – 61.52% return**

December 14, 2017
Distribution $3.42 x 980.5057 = $3353.33
Shares reinvested: 40.3870
Total shares owned: 1020.8927

December 29, 2017
Net asset value: 84.33
**IRA value: $86,091.88 – 95.66% return**

December 13, 2018
Distribution $5.55 x 1020.8927 = $5669.22
Shares reinvested: 79.2898
Total shares owned: 1100.1825

December 31, 2018
Net asset value: $68.29
**IRA value: $75131.46– 70.75% return**

# Diversified Mutual Fund

Mutual Fund:  **Janus Henderson Balanced (JABAX)**
Investment Category:  Mixed Target
                        Allocation: Moderate
Maximum Front End Sales Load: No Load

June 1, 2017
Max IRA purchases: $6500)
$31.55 net asset value
Total 206.0222 shares owned.

September 29, 2017
Distribution $.14 x 206.0222 = $28.84
Shares reinvested: 0.8877
Total shares owned: 206.9099

December 19, 2017
Distribution $1.30 x 206.9099 = $268.98
Shares reinvested: 8.1634
Total shares owned: 215.0733

December 29, 2017
Net asset value: $32.89
Total investment: $6500
**IRA value: $7073.76 – 8.83% return**

March 29, 2018
Distribution $.12 x 206.9099 = $24.83
Shares reinvested: 0.7533
Total shares owned: 215.8266

June 29, 2018
Distribution $.12 x 215.8266 = $25.90
Shares reinvested: 0.7690
Total shares owned: 216.5956

September 28, 2018
Distribution $.11 x 216.5956 = $23.83
Shares reinvested: 0.6759
Total shares owned: 217.2715

December 18, 2018
Distribution $1.80 x 217.2715 = $391.09
Shares reinvested: 12.5914
Total shares owned: 229.8629

December 31, 2018
Net asset value: $30.93
**IRA value: $7109.66 – 9.38% return**

### Another Diversified Mutual Fund

Mutual Fund: **Fidelity Selects: Utility Growth (FSUTX)**

Investment Category: Utility
Maximum Front End Sales Load: No Load

June 1, 2018
Max IRA purchases: $6500)
$82.43 net asset value
Total 78.8548 shares owned.

December 14, 2018
Distribution $6.46 x 78.8548 = $509.40
Shares reinvested: 5.9916
Total shares owned: 84.8464

December 31, 2018
Net asset value: $80.12
**IRA value: $6797.89 – 4.58% return**

**As of December 31, 2018:**

1. **IRA value:  $75131.46**
2. **IRA value:  $7109.66**
3. **IRA value:  $6797.89**

**$89,039.01 – 56.21%**
**total return on investments**

To demonstrate how quickly the market changes, the following IRA values are established on the net asset values as a March 15, 2019:

1. Net asset value is $71.80 x 1100.1825 equals IRA value: $78,993.10
2. net asset value is $33.42 x 229.8629 equals IRA value: $7682.02
3. net asset value is $87.94 x 84.8464 equals IRA value: $7461.39

   $94,136.51 – 65.15%
   total return on investments

www.ingramcontent.com/pod-product-compliance
Lightning Source LLC
Chambersburg PA
CBHW080900170526
45158CB00012B/2868